D1519442

Saint Joseph

Under the direction of Romain Lizé, CEO, MAGNIFICAT
Editor, MAGNIFICAT: Isabelle Galmiche
Editor, Ignatius: Vivian Dudro
Proofreader: Kathleen Hollenbeck
Artistic Designers: Armelle Riva, Gauthier Delauné
Production: Thierry Dubus, Sabine Marioni

Scripture quotations are from Revised Standard Version of the Bible–Second Catholic
Edition (Ignatius Edition). Copyright © 2006 by the National Council of the Churches of
Christ in the United States of America. Used by permission. All rights reserved.

Original French edition: *Saint Joseph, protège notre famille*
© Mame, Paris, 2021

© 2021 by MAGNIFICAT, New York • Ignatius Press, San Francisco
All rights reserved
ISBN Ignatius Press 978-1-62164-513-9 • ISBN MAGNIFICAT 978-1-949239-61-4
The trademark MAGNIFICAT depicted in this publication is used under license from
and is the exclusive property of MAGNIFICAT Central Service Team, Inc., A Ministry to
Catholic Women and may not be used without its written consent.

Sabine du Mesnil ✶ Hengjing Zang

Saint Joseph

Watch Over My Family

MAGNIFICAT · Ignatius

Contents

· PART 1 ·
Who Is Saint Joseph?

· PART 2 ·
Learn from Saint Joseph

· PART 3 ·

Prayers and Stories

Who Is Saint Joseph?

Joseph, Chosen by God

God is so great that he wished to be close to everyone by giving the world his Son, Jesus.

To accomplish this great plan of love, God chose Mary, wholly pure, to be Jesus' mother. And he chose Joseph, a just man, to be the guardian of Mary and Jesus.

Joseph was engaged to Mary, and they both lived in Nazareth. The name Nazareth is said to have come from a word that means "to watch over." And that was Joseph's role: to protect God's treasures, Mary and Jesus. He became the husband of Mary and the father of Jesus on earth.

Joseph was a descendant of King David, from whose family the Son of God, the promised Savior, was to come. Thanks to Joseph this prophecy was fulfilled! When the Christ Child was born, his parents named him Jesus, which means "God saves."

Like Noah and Abraham before him, Joseph was a just man. He was kind to his neighbor and sought to love God in everything he did. He is often depicted in paintings with a beard, a symbol of his maturity and wisdom.

Joseph, Craftsman

Joseph lived by the work of his hands. He was a carpenter. This trade requires not only strength to work the wood, but also know-how, perseverance, and care.

When Joseph chose the wood of the olive tree, and when he tenderly handled the wood of the elm, he could see its hidden potential to become a work of art. Joseph knew what was hidden inside. And his craftsman's eye prepared him for the beautiful mission entrusted to him by God: to raise Jesus, hidden and unnoticed, until the time came for his mission to begin. Joseph probably taught Jesus the skills of carpentry too!

Carpenters build not only tables and chairs, but also houses. Joseph built a house for the Son of God on earth. And Jesus came to earth to establish an eternal dwelling for us in heaven.

As we await heaven, God is here among us in many places. He is with us in churches, tabernacles, and the hearts of all friends of God!

The risen Jesus promised us: "I am with you every day until the end of time." Ever since he ascended to heaven, Jesus has kept that promise—every day for thousands of years! He doesn't want to be separated from us for one single moment. What an extraordinary gift of love!

"Joseph, Do Not Fear!"

When Joseph was engaged to Mary, he learned that she was expecting a child who was not his own. What a shock! Joseph didn't know if he could trust Mary.

Then, one night, an angel visited him to announce good news: the child Mary carried was the Son of God!

The angel told Joseph to take Mary into his home without fear. And without question, he obeyed.

"Joseph, son of David, do not fear to take Mary your wife [into your home], for that which is conceived in her is of the Holy Spirit; she will bear a son, and you shall call his name Jesus, for he will save his people from their sins." . . . When Joseph woke from sleep, he did as the angel of the Lord commanded him; he took his wife [into his home].

Matthew 1:20-21; 24

God Trusted Joseph

Joseph showed great courage in doing what God asked of him. Trusting in God, Joseph was unafraid of making difficult decisions. He worked hard to be the husband of Mary and the earthly father of Jesus.

When it came time for Mary to give birth, Joseph and Mary traveled to Bethlehem. Mary needed help and comfort, but there was no room at the inn. Joseph found a place for Mary in a humble stable. He lit a fire to keep her warm. He fetched water and tidied up a manger to serve as a cradle for baby Jesus.

Joseph was the first one to present Jesus to the world when he welcomed the shepherds and the magi who came to see the Christ Child.

God knew he could count on Joseph. He trusted in him and in the many talents he had given him.

You, too, are full of talents that God has given you. He counts on you to put them to good use as you place your trust in him.

In quietness and in trust shall be your strength.
Isaiah 30:15

"Joseph, Rise!"

Joseph's life wasn't always easy.

King Herod wanted to kill baby Jesus so that he would remain the only king. To protect the child from Herod's wrath, an angel told Joseph to leave everything behind and flee to Egypt, a foreign land. It was dark outside. Joseph probably would have liked to wait until morning. But instead, he set Mary and Jesus on a donkey and left in the night without looking back. Mary, too, did not complain; she trusted Joseph.

Much later, an angel spoke to him once again: "Rise, take the child and his mother." Joseph obeyed and returned to his country.

Twice an angel came to Joseph to light up the night with the word "Rise!", which also means "Rise again to life! Flee the dark night of fear!" In the midst of all his difficulties, Joseph rose and took Mary and Jesus with him, trusting that God was always there by his side.

And you, too, have nothing to fear if you pray to Saint Joseph and take Mary and Jesus into your home and your heart.

Joseph, Shadow of God the Father

Silence surrounds the life of Saint Joseph from beginning to end. When was he born? How old was he at the time of the birth of Jesus? No one knows. Saint Joseph was completely discreet and humble. He always put Jesus first and placed himself at his service.

Love is patient and kind;
love is not jealous or boastful.

1 Corinthians 13:4

It's sometimes said that Joseph is the "earthly shadow of our heavenly Father."

This means that Saint Joseph was an image of the presence of God as he fulfilled his fatherly role in the life of Jesus.

Does a shadow seek to shine? Is it a blinding light? No, but when it's hot outside, a shadow is soothing! It's a place where we can find shelter, refreshment, and rest. Just so was the home Saint Joseph provided for Jesus.

*Jesus is a hidden treasure...
and to find something hidden, one must hide oneself.
We must resemble Jesus, whose face was hidden.*

Saint Thérèse of Lisieux

Joseph, a Man Who Listened

God speaks softly—in the gentle breeze, in the whispers of angels. In order to hear him, we must learn to be silent. Joseph was a man of silence, a man who listened. Not one word from Joseph is reported in the Bible.

Mary and Joseph didn't tell the whole village that Jesus was the Son of God. They remained silent, listening for God's word and waiting for him to guide them.

Many times, Jesus was a mystery to Mary and Joseph, and in their amazement they remained silent. When they presented baby Jesus in the Temple, and the old priest Simeon foretold that Jesus would be the light of the world, Joseph and Mary said nothing and marveled at the priest's words.

Sometimes Mary and Joseph did not understand Jesus completely, as when Jesus was lost and found in the Temple at twelve years old. When he asked Mary and Joseph, "Did you not know that I must be in my Father's house?", Jesus meant his Father in heaven of course! However, the Gospels tell us that Jesus "went down with them and came to Nazareth, and was obedient to them."

A Father Who Teaches

Joseph's name means "to increase," and "to make grow." To help Jesus grow up, Saint Joseph protected him. He gave Jesus a zest for work well done, work useful to others and carried out with a smile. And he taught him to respect the laws of the land.

Joseph also taught Jesus salvation history and the Scriptures. And he showed Jesus by example how to follow the will of God.

You shall love the LORD, your God, with all your heart, and with all your soul, and with all your might.

And these words which I command you this day shall be upon your heart; and you shall teach them diligently to your children.
Deuteronomy 6:5-7

It's not known exactly when Joseph died. Saint Joseph was by Jesus' side during his hidden life in Nazareth, preparing him for his mission to proclaim the good news of salvation.

By the time Jesus began his public life, Joseph had died.

It is believed that Joseph died with Jesus and Mary by his side. What a beautiful and peaceful death. That is why Saint Joseph is known as the "patron of a happy death," to whom people often pray for their dying loved ones.

The Holy Family

Joseph was a loving, caring father. Mary was a mother full of tenderness. And Jesus was a loving and beloved child!

We call the family they formed the Holy Family. The three of them loved one another so much that they were of one single heart. At the same time, they had great respect for one another; they all remained uniquely themselves!

That is the same mystery of the love within the Trinity: Father, Son, and Holy Spirit, one God in Three Persons. The Holy Family was united as an image of the Trinity on earth. The Holy Family shows us that love within a family is an image of the love within God himself.

Come, Holy Spirit, Spirit of love and peace!

PART 2

Learn from Saint Joseph

An Extraordinary Patron Saint!

Saint Joseph is a patron saint for many people. The whole world can take refuge under his immense cloak! In particular, Saint Joseph protects:
- fathers
- families, both united and broken
- men and women seeking to marry
- couples hoping for a child
- the poor, refugees, and exiles
- those looking for a new home, and those who are homeless
- workers, and those who have lost their jobs
- monks, nuns, priests, and all who consecrate their lives to God

- those who are near death
- the whole Church (Saint Joseph is the patron of the universal Church.)
- everyone named Joseph

Saint Joseph,
today I entrust (mention name of person or family) to you
Be for us a model of love
and of courage in difficult times.

Think of Saint Joseph!

To think about and pray to Saint Joseph, it helps to have a small picture, an icon, or a statue of him. If you don't already have one, turn to page 43 in this book: you can make a copy of this picture and place it in your prayer corner or on your desk. Now you're ready to draw near to him in your thought and prayer.

Like people on pilgrimage to a shrine, you can write a letter to Saint Joseph telling him about your intentions, your worries, your joys. He will carry them in his prayers before God. You can slip it beneath his statue or his picture. It can be a long letter, just a little note, or even a drawing! Saint Joseph will see your act of faith and will listen to you.

Have no anxiety about anything,
but in everything by prayer ... with thanksgiving
let your requests be made known to God.

Philippians 4:6

In the School of Silence

God is there for you in the silence. You can ask Saint Joseph to teach you how to keep silent in order to hear the Lord better.

Here are a few ideas to help you.

You can take just a moment of silence before switching on the computer or the TV, or before going out to play with others. These little moments of silence are precious. At first, the silence may seem empty and difficult! But God is there, waiting in the secret of your heart. Little by little, you'll be able to feel God's presence and his peace.

You can go to a church to meet Jesus in adoration. Joseph built a house for Jesus on earth, and today, Jesus is still present in the tabernacles of Catholic churches. You can kneel before him and softly say, "You are here and you love me. Thank you, Jesus!"

I have calmed and quieted my soul,
like a child quieted at its mother's breasts;
like a child that is quieted is my soul.
Psalm 131:2

The Faithful Servant

With great discretion, Saint Joseph made sure that Mary and Jesus wanted for nothing. He was there for them every day.

Following the example of Saint Joseph, you too can be helpful in small, secret ways:
· empty the dishwasher without having to be asked
· put away toys lying around the living room
· help your little sister get dressed
· give your mom a smile when she wakes you up in the morning
· pick a little bouquet of flowers to put on the table
· slip a loving note under your dad's pillow
· try to think of other ways to be helpful

You'll soon see: being helpful in secret brings happiness!

To pick up a pin for love of God can convert a soul.
Saint Thérèse of Lisieux

Do Not Be Afraid!

In trust, Joseph obeyed the angel. He knew he could count on God. And you? Like Joseph, don't hesitate to say, "My God, I trust in you!"

Sometimes, there may be things that worry you. Perhaps you are moving to a new house, maybe your mom or dad is out of work. Or maybe a friend or family member is very sick. Give your cares to Saint Joseph, and he will intercede for you. He will bring your needs to God and pray on your behalf.

Don't hesitate to make very practical requests. He listens to the smallest detail of your prayers. Are you hoping for a bedroom all to yourself? Tell Saint Joseph.

Is your dad working long hours and you'd like to see him more often? Talk to Saint Joseph about it! Your aunt is hoping to get married? Entrust that to Saint Joseph too!

You'll see: Saint Joseph likes to help us out as he works to make God known and loved.

The Tenderness of a Father

Saint Joseph was the husband of the Blessed Virgin Mary and the father of Jesus on earth. Entrust your dad to him when you pray the "Hail, Joseph," either once a week, in a novena, or every day! You can also pray for all dads. Being a father is a great joy, but it isn't always easy. Saint Joseph both sets an example for fathers everywhere and prays for them.

You can also ask Saint Joseph to help you as you grow up. He was meek and humble as a child. And he became one of the greatest saints in heaven!

In Nazareth, Saint Joseph repaired broken houses and damaged roofs. Today, he can help repair your broken heart, your sorrows, and your wounds. Don't be afraid of your weaknesses, for your Father in heaven looks upon them with tenderness.

There is only one you in the world, and God has given you many hidden talents. Ask Saint Joseph to help you discover and develop them! You are capable of great and wonderful things!

You are precious in my eyes, ... and I love you.
Isaiah 43:4

Let's Get Going!

Joseph was a man on the go! He traveled the roads from Nazareth to Bethlehem with his pregnant wife, Mary. Then he left Bethlehem for Egypt. He must have walked more than a hundred hours to get there! Then, still on foot, he walked all the way back to Nazareth.

Following in his footsteps, you could suggest that your family set off on a pilgrimage. That would be a good time to entrust all your intentions to Saint Joseph.

Here are a few pilgrimage sites you could visit.

Wherever you are, there is likely a parish church dedicated to Saint Joseph nearby. You can make a mini-pilgrimage by visiting that church.

If you live in the western United States, you might make a pilgrimage to one of the Franciscan missions between San Diego and Sonoma, California. There is even one named for Saint Joseph: Mission San Jose in Fremont. In Santa Fe, New Mexico, many people visit the Loretto Chapel to see the marvelous spiral staircase that seems to defy the laws of physics. It was built by a mysterious carpenter some people believe was Saint Joseph in disguise. (See the story on p. 52.)

On the other side of the country is the National Shrine of the North American Martyrs in Auriesville, New York. It is dedicated to three Jesuit missionaries who were killed by hostile natives in the 1600s. During an influenza epidemic, these Jesuits prayed a novena to Saint Joseph, whom they considered their faithful guardian.

About three hundred miles north of there, in Montreal, Quebec, is the largest shrine in the world dedicated to Saint Joseph: Saint Joseph's Oratory of Mount Royal. Its founder, Holy Cross brother Saint André Bessette, had a lifelong devotion to Saint Joseph.

The Basilica of the National Shrine of the Immaculate Conception, in Washington, D.C., is a great place to pray during a visit to the nation's capital. It is named for the patroness of the United States, Mary, under her title of the Immaculate Conception. Saint Joseph is honored throughout the basilica in mosaics, stained glass, and sculptures.

Prayers
and Stories

Hail, Joseph

Hail, Joseph, filled with divine grace,
in whose arms the Savior was carried
and under whose eyes he grew up:
blessed are you among men
and blessed is Jesus, the Son of your dear Spouse.

Holy Joseph, chosen to be a father to the Son of God,
pray for us in the midst of our cares
of family, health, and work,
and be pleased to assist us at the hour of our death.
Amen.

Blessed Are You, Joseph!

Blessed are you among men,
and blessed are your eyes
that have seen the Savior;
blessed are your ears
that heard the voice of the angel;
blessed are your hands
that touched the Son of God;
blessed are your arms
that carried him who carries the world;
blessed is your chest
on which the Son of God rested his head;
blessed is your heart
burning with love for Jesus;
blessed is the angel
who served as your guardian;
blessed for ever
are all those who love and bless you.
Amen.

Based on a prayer by Saint John Eudes

A Novena to Saint Joseph

Each day for nine days, read the sentence suggested below. Then offer your prayer petition and recite the "Hail, Joseph" or the "Blessed Are You, Joseph." Saint Joseph will be attentive to your act of faith.

First day: Saint Joseph, friend of God and of little ones, watch over me.

Second day: Saint Joseph, pure of heart, make me meek and humble of heart.

Third day: Saint Joseph, man of dreams, guardian of prayer, teach me how to pray.

Fourth day: Saint Joseph, husband of Mary, help me to do the will of the Father.

Fifth day: Saint Joseph, exiled in Egypt, protector of the family, pray for our families.

Sixth day: Saint Joseph of Nazareth, model of workers, help me to build the Kingdom of God.

Seventh day: Saint Joseph, protector of the Church, help me to avoid evil and to love the Body of Christ.

Eighth day: Saint Joseph, man of silence, teach me how to be silent and generous.

Ninth day: Saint Joseph, fatherly and merciful of heart, come to the aid of all the lost sheep.

You can then end your novena by reciting a few litanies to Saint Joseph.

Saint Joseph, pray for us.
Joseph, most just, pray for us.
Joseph, most chaste, pray for us.
Joseph, most prudent, pray for us.
Joseph, most strong, pray for us.
Joseph, most obedient, pray for us.
Joseph, most faithful, pray for us.

Prayer for the Morning

O glorious Saint Joseph,
who watched over Jesus and Mary,
protect me this day.
Grant me a pure heart and stillness
so that I can hear the voice of God.
I entrust to you my thoughts and my deeds,
my sorrows and my joys,
that, this evening, I may give praise to God with you!
Amen.

Prayer before Sleeping

Saint Joseph,
who was peacefully sleeping
when Herod threatened;
who heard the voice of the angel
as you slept:
grant that I may not fear
the night and the darkness;
grant that I may sleep
in peace this night.
Amen.

Prayer for a Journey

Saint Joseph,
trusting in God, you set off on a journey
with no questions asked,
seeking only
to save the Child Jesus.
Watch over me and my family
during this journey.
Accompany us
as we set out and as we return.
Thank you, Saint Joseph.
Amen.

Prayer to the Holy Family

Jesus, Mary, and Joseph,
in you we contemplate
the splendor of true love,
and we pray to you with confidence.

Holy Family of Nazareth,
make of our families
places of communion and prayer,
schools of the Gospel,
and little domestic churches.

Holy Family of Nazareth,
teach us how to love,
to forgive, and to live in peace.
Comfort those who weep,
heal those who are ill.
Jesus, Mary, and Joseph,
hear us and grant our prayer.
Amen.

Based on a prayer by Pope Francis

The Miraculous Staircase

A group of nuns settled in Santa Fe, New Mexico. They entrusted building work to the protection of Saint Joseph, whom they particularly honored. A school was built first, and then a chapel. It was all wonderful, but in the chapel the builders had forgotten to put in a staircase to the choir loft! How would anyone get up there? Climbing such a tall ladder would be too dangerous. The sisters began praying a novena to Saint Joseph. On the last day of the novena, a gray-haired man appeared at the door with three tools. He offered his help and set to work. Seven months later, there stood a marvelous winding staircase. It rose up with no central support other than its own tightly turned pieces. It was constructed with wood of an unknown species, and the old man had disappeared without a trace. The sisters were convinced it was Saint Joseph himself who had built their staircase! For 150 years, pilgrims have flocked to the site to admire the staircase and to pray to Saint Joseph.

Good Saint Joseph

The Little Sisters of the Poor care for the elderly poor. As one Christmas approached, they dreamt of offering treats to the residents of their house, but they had none to give. So they entrusted this concern to Saint Joseph. With that, someone rang at the door bearing a box of candied fruits. To their great surprise, there was just the right number of candies for each one of the residents.

One day, there were barely enough logs left to put on the fire to keep warm. They presented their need to Saint Joseph. One sister decided to go ask a man who wasn't normally in the habit of assisting them. The sister stated with confidence, "I asked Saint Joseph for it."

The man teased her, saying, "And do you think Saint Joseph is going to come down from heaven to deliver it in person?"

"No," replied the sister, "he'll make use of some nice, charitable person to bring it to us." Moved by her confidence, the man had a large load of logs delivered to her door! Saint Joseph likes to involve everyone in his little miracles!

Down to the Last Detail

The Little Sisters of the Poor entrust all their wants and needs to Saint Joseph in prayer. They trust in him, and Saint Joseph always grants their prayers down to the last detail!

In Algeria, the Little Sisters of the Poor slipped a picture of a van under the statue of Saint Joseph. They fervently prayed to him; they really wanted that vehicle! In the picture, the van had no window or back seat. But that was no matter; Saint Joseph would understand! Saint Joseph answered their prayers with humor: the nuns did indeed receive a van—but it had no window and no back seat!

One day, another group of sisters each wrote a request to Saint Joseph on a piece of paper. But one of them didn't know how to write, so she drew a picture of a horse. It turned out nicely, but there wasn't enough room on the paper for her to draw the tail. A few days later, a local farmer brought the nuns a horse. "I thought he could be of use to you," the man said. "As you see, he lost his tail in an accident, but he's still a very good horse!"

Printed in in February 2021, in Poland, by Dimograf.
Job number MGN21016
Printed in compliance with the Consumer
Protection Safety Act, 2008